J.B. NWANKWO:  MEMORANDUM TO PRONACO

# MEMORANDUM

# TO

# PRONACO

BY

## J. B. NWANKWO

First published May 25, 2009





ISBN 978-1-906914-24-0


Other Public Policy Books by Ben Nnolim Books

| Title | Paperback | Hardback | eBook |
| --- | --- | --- | --- |
| In Search of Order | 978-1-906914-00-4 | 978-1-906914-63-9 | 978-1-906914-33-2 |
| Technological Emancipation of Nigeria, The Role of Chemical Engineering | 978-1-906914-18-9 | | 978-1-906914-34-9 |
| Memorandum to PRONACO | 978-1-906914-24-0 | | 978-1-906914-35-6 |


Ben Nnolim Books,
7 Sandway Path,
St. Mary Cray,
Orpington, Kent
BR5 3TS

# PREFACE

One cynic was reported to have said that seminars and workshops, and by implication conferences, were talk shops for professional windbags. This may be true of some conferences, especially in some academic circles, but certainly not true of the Berlin (Congo) Conference of 1884-1885 and of the various constitutional conferences that led to the political independence of many African countries between the 1940s and the 1960s.

National conferences have degenerated, in Nigeria since the first *coup de etat* of 1966, from serious affairs in which serious national issues were seriously addressed to jamborees and talk shops for professional and non-professional windbags in which the issues were of less importance than the appearance of tackling them. The matter has reached the stage where public figures indeed consider the problem solved once a national conference, seminar or workshop on the problem has been successfully organised.

There have been many national conferences, workshops and seminars on various national issues throughout the regimes of General Jack Gowon, General Murtala Mohamed, General Olusegun Obasanjo, Alhaji Shehu Shagari, General Muhamadu Buhari, General Badamosi Babangida, General Sani Abacha, Chief Olusegun Obasanjo and Alhaji Musa Yar Adua. Each of them has had one common thread running through them, namely, the heavy use of social climbing and unscrupulous academics some of who, eventually, turn up as government ministers, vice chancellors of universities, director generals, etc. Each national conference, seminar or workshop has had the consequence of not really addressing, satisfactorily, the particular national issues which it set out to address.

When General Obasanjo set up or was planning to set up another national conference in 2004, popularly known, then, as Obasanjo's Confab, Chief Anthony Enahoro and Professor Wole

Soyinka were reported to be setting up a parallel conference because they felt that Obasanjo's Confab had started with the *a priori* weakness of having no-go areas. Their forum was a temporary organisation known as PRONACO.

It is not clear now whether this PRONACO conference eventually took place as it was reported that the federal government was making moves to deal with the objections, of the PRONACO group, to the terms of reference of the Obasanjo Confab. Perhaps they were talked out of holding the conference.

This book, MEMORANDUM TO PRONACO, is a publication of the memorandum sent to Chief Anthony Enahoro's group because it was the group that had intended, even if the conference never took place, to deal objectively with the most cogent national issues of the day.

The problems this memorandum discussed in 2004 are still with us, some resulting in violent conflict, some hidden under the carpet, some gestating to rise up later, some getting superficial and some getting military, authoritarian, treatment. This, I suppose, is the fate of nations. The fight, call it work, has to go on.

J. B. Nwankwo

24 May, 2009

# DEDICATION

This book is dedicated to all Africans, south of the Sahara, who are living, suffering and dying in artificial countries.

# TABLE OF CONTENTS

# CHAPTER ONE
# GENERAL COMMENTS ON OBASANJO'S CONFAB

The first obvious comment is that the fact that President Obasanjo finally agreed to a national conference, colloquially referred to as a confab, and, actually, organized one, for whatever reason, shows, clearly, that President Obasanjo's government and the national assembly, since 1999, like their predecessors, have failed the nation.

Nigerians, reeling from many years of inept, corrupt and disastrous military rule, expected the "democratic" government of President Obasanjo and the national assembly to quickly tackle the fundamental problems of resource mismanagement, salary and pension arrears, debts to local contractors, dilapidated or out of date infrastructure and unjust and inequitable treatment of ethnic majorities and minorities.

Laws reinforcing and clarifying fundamental human rights, rights to dissent, rights of abode, etc, were expected to have been quickly passed and enforced. It is some of these neglected items that the Obasanjo Confab should have been set up to address. And it was only when President Obasanjo set up his Confab that the national assembly realized that this was its province. All this is a big indictment on the new "democratic" government since 1999.

The second comment is that Obasanjo's Confab has turned out, like previous similar conferences, to be a waste of time and another gross misuse of the nation's resources of money and manpower. Earlier, President Obasanjo had set up a committee to review the 1999 constitution and so did the national assembly. Each of these committees spent a considerable amount of money, time, etc., going around the country, ostensibly, to collect input for the review.

The same President Obasanjo set up the Oputa Panel., which was received with enthusiasm and very great participation by Nigerians. Panel members put in all they had and showcased the great talents and resource persons Nigeria had. After all the money spent, the energy put in by everybody, nothing has come out of either the constitution review committees or from the Oputa Panel. The way things have gone, nothing will come out of President Obasanjo's latest Confab.

The resources employed for this Confab could have been better applied to paying local contractors (thus increasing employment and waking up our comatose economy), medical doctors (who were recently, or are still, on strike), pensioners and improving facilities in our educational and health institutions.

The history of national/constitutional conferences in Nigeria, since after the Nigerian civil war, has been that the delegates use them as opportunities to forge alliances for the formation of new political parties for the next dispensation and, usually, produce faulty, part-baked documents with flaws and loopholes which they hope to exploit when their party comes into power. The failure of pre-Independence conferences could be blamed on the undue influences from Britain and the colonial powers. Post independence, we have no excuse.

The third comment is that Nigerians are not ready for a national conference in spite of all the noise. The parties clamouring for a conference are, often, self or military regime appointed or created leaders or those that are out of favour with the regime in power angling for relevance and recognition. They do not have hard historical, anthropological, political, economic, religious and other information or statistics sufficient to make any credible case for their positions except part-baked opinions based on ethnic or other sentiment or prejudice and on playing to the gallery.

Despite the numbers of professors of history, political science, anthropology, economics and management, and the many disciplines and institutes in our universities there are no serious studies, dissertations, theses or books in our universities, polytechnics, colleges of education or institutes that anybody can refer to, to obtain objective background information for discourse on the national question. What is more common is that these academics will show up as resource persons to these parties and pass off, as intellectual input, hastily prepared subjective opinion whose main criteria for acceptability is that it supports the position of the party that engaged them and from whom they expect the reward of some public appointment.

# CHAPTER TWO
## NATIONAL CONFERENCES

A country does not go to the type of national conference, such as Obasanjo's Confab, to discuss political parties and other such mundane items listed by Mr. President.

A national conference arises, usually, because of crisis or because the parties involved have reached the stage in which only two options are left – dialogue or war. The very things President Obasanjo listed as no-go areas are, often, what a national conference is, always, about. These can be summarized as follows:

1. whether the component units should continue their association (national unity or disunity) and on what terms (federation, confederation or friendly neighbouring countries)
2. the economic model of the association including resource control and income/wealth distribution
3. the place of religion in national and public affairs in the association

Parties to a national conference, usually, have clout and a following so that there is a clear balance of power or terror. A national conference is, usually, convened or facilitated by third or neutral parties or by the contending parties themselves.

History, both ancient and modern, is replete with various forms, origins and consequences of national conferences. Countries with such histories include the UK, Switzerland, Belgium, Canada, USA, India/Pakistan, Pakistan/Bangladesh, Yugoslavia, USSR, Indonesia/East Timor, to name only a few. Decisions reached at national conferences are such that, if not implemented, usually, a war results or at best, everyone runs back to the trenches.

Obasanjo's Confab

When Obasanjo's Confab is viewed against what has been written above, it becomes clear that, although there have been crisis of one form or another in Nigeria for a long time, none of the protesting parties believes so strongly in its cause or is cohesive enough to carry its protest or objection to a logical conclusion. Each will make a lot of noise, burn properties or even go to war as the Igbos did but as soon as it encounters serious challenge; it quickly loses steam and acquiesces in a status worse than the one it fought to remove. Compare this to the Vietnamese, the Kenyan, the Eritrean and recently, the Ukranian situations.

President Obasanjo, the convener of this confab, is neither a neutral nor objective party. He is more like Colonel Nicholson (played by Alec Guinness) in the film "The Bridge on River Kwai" who forgot that there was a war going on in his quest to show their Japanese captors how disciplined British soldiers were. President Obasanjo is so obsessed with Nigerian unity that he has forgotten that countries are made by and for human beings and not the other way round and that the emancipation of the black man, especially in Africa, will not happen, ever, using the structures put in place by white colonialists.

None of the participants in Obasanjo's Confab, except perhaps the Muslims and not even President Obasanjo himself, has any clout or following. For as long as there is no balance of power or terror among the participants, the confab is just a jamboree and an opportunity for the participants to let out steam and earn some honorarium and largesse at the nation's expense.

The National Conference Nigeria should have, if It has to

There is an Igbo saying that the footpath created by your neighbour, behind or beside your house, can never be closed unless there is a fight between the two of you over it. Even if he beat you to a pulp the first time you challenged him, when he thinks of the labour involved in beating you up again, because you will challenge him again, he will choose to take another route and avoid the path under dispute.

A near English interpretation of this Igbo saying is that nobody gives you freedom because if freedom is given to you, it can, also, be taken away from you. Thus when Nigerian journalists ask for press freedom, academicians for academic freedom and professionals for freedom to be professionals, it is clear that they are not serious in their demand.

Thus, President Obasanjo's confab is not a national confab at all. He has merely invited his friends, associates and their collaborators to help him polish his idea of what he thinks Nigeria ought to be. If ethnic, professional, religious or any groups want a confab, they, and not the government, are the proper persons to call such a confab either among themselves or with groups they would like to discuss with. With current ethnic organizations largely peopled and managed by social climbers and megalomaniacs whose major vision is themselves and the power and wealth they would acquire if they manage to be seen as champions of their ethnic interests, any national conference in Nigeria, right now, will, not only be a waste of time but also, a major retrogressive step backwards.

So, if there is no national conference, how can Nigerians discuss and solve their problems? I will attempt to address this question later but, first of all, let us agree on what the issues should be.

# CHAPTER THREE
# ISSUES THAT MUST BE ADDRESSED IN NIGERIA

There are three issues that need urgent, honest and objective discussion in Nigeria. These are

1.  the unity and indivisibility of Nigeria
2.  resource control and income/wealth distribution
3.  religion and secularity in Nigeria

<u>Unity and Indivisibility of Nigeria</u>

One of the most amazing statements made in Nigeria by public officials and increasingly echoed by the mass media are

1.  Nigeria is greater than all of us
2.  We have no other country to go to than Nigeria

People who make the first statement know that the Atlantic ocean and the Sahara desert are not members of the United Nations and do not feature in the Olympics or World Cup in any game because there are no people there. Instead, they can be subjects of dispute of ownership by countries and nations made up of people. It is people who make up nations and countries not the other way around. And those countries that become nations do so because the smallest living human being is their most important component.

Some of us may remember when the German government sent a chartered plane to Jos to convey back to Germany, one German who caught *lassa* fever in Jos, Nigeria. We may also remember when the Nigerian Air Force was carrying out exercises somewhere near Lagos and killed a little boy by accident. The Chief of Air Staff, then, dismissed it, nonchalantly, as one of those things and nothing was done about it. Yet, it is because of that little boy and every single citizen that Nigeria maintains, at very great expense, an Air Force.

The history of nations and the world illustrate clearly that any geographical expression, in which the inhabitants are not more important than that expression, has never been, cannot be and will never be, a nation. It will continue to be called a country just as Nigeria continues to be called a country but not a nation.

Those who say that we have no other country to go to cannot be unaware of the many Nigerians who are naturalizing in other countries and even foreigners who are angling to be Nigerian citizens. Even without naturalizing, many Nigerians are spending their lifetimes in other countries with some not even wanting to visit Nigeria. The long and short of it is that we have two hundred and twenty three other countries (according to the United Nations) to go to if we wish. And our young people, finding that Nigeria has nothing for them, are leaving the country in droves.

The mass media and anybody, who reads newspapers, magazines, listens to the radio or has gone to school up to school certificate level, knows about the amalgamation of northern and southern Nigeria by the British and perhaps, their reasons for doing so. People who have given it some thought know that this amalgamation of backward peoples with conflicting cultures served British interests at the time and, luckily for them, in modern times, continues to serve their present interest of ensuring that the black man continues to be backward and dependent on European and American interests.

Is it fair, now that we are in control of our affairs, to make people who have one known life time, regardless of what those who believe in re-incarnation think, to throw their lives away building what their so called leaders keep calling a great nation, which history, and all right thinking people, know will never happen under these circumstances.

Our so called leaders throw about the jargon, unity in diversity, to enable them evade the obvious conclusions from every day events happening before their very eyes. What diversity (tribe, language, religion, culture) do we have in Nigeria that makes us one nation that cannot be found between us and our neighbouring countries, Cameroon, Chad, Mali, Niger, Togo, Benin and even far away places like Kenya, Uganda, etc? Do Nigerians not live, work and trade in these countries without fewer beheadings, looting of their shops and seizing their "abandoned" properties than in their so called country? What is wrong with being citizens of friendly, neighbouring countries with certainty of recourse to international law when aggrieved than being citizens of one country without recourse to any justice or law?

Our so called leaders often boast about Nigeria being the giant of Africa. The basis of the boast is our large population (about 137 million, see Table 1) and our vast natural resources. All the statistics, however, show us as disgraceful wastrels, thieves and scoundrels that are among the world's most poor. It is not just statistics alone. Ask any Nigerian, high or low, he will not only confirm the statistics but also give you even more. When do we stop deceiving ourselves?

The United Nations recognizes the existence of two hundred and twenty four countries as of mid-2004. Out of these, 51.3% have populations less than 5 million. Ireland's population is less than four million. Another 15.6% have populations between 5 and 10 million. Another 6.7 % have populations between 10 and 15 million while another 4.9 % have populations between 15 and 20 million. As you go on, you find that 84.4 % of the countries of the world have populations less than 30 million. Only 15.6 % of the countries of the world have populations above 30 million. Of these, only five countries, or 2.2%, have population between 100 and 150 million – Japan (127 million), Nigeria (137 million), Bangladesh (141 million), Russia (144 million) and Pakistan (159 million). Another five countries, or 2.2%, have population above 150 million – Brazil (184 million), Indonesia (238 million), United States (293 million), India (1.065 billion) and China (1.298 billion).

Space does not allow presentation of detailed analysis of this matter but the point is that Nigeria does not have the historical, managerial or technological background or expertise to manage its large, under-developed and conflictingly diverse population. No country in the developed world contains more than two language groups or cultures. No country can get anywhere when many of its citizens do not understand each others' language or culture.

The best option for Nigeria (and indeed Africa south of the Sahara) and for the future of the black man is for Nigeria (and indeed the current African countries south of the Sahara) to break up into friendly, one or two language, neighbouring countries than continue to believe this pipe dream of making anything meaningful out of the 250 diverse ethnic groups.

Keeping Nigeria one for the reason that non-oil producing areas will be disadvantaged disregards the facts on the ground in pursuit of a short sighted and European inspired point of view. No group of countries carved out of Nigeria will starve, as human and material resources of great value are evenly distributed among them.

If size is our problem, we can get at least ten viable countries with an average population of about 13 to 14 million, which, with the associated resources, will still make each of those countries a force to be reckoned with both in Africa and the rest of the world. As can be seen in Figures 1 to 5, 70 % of African countries, in 2004, had populations less than 15 million while 80% had population less than 27 million (see also, Table 1). Population is not static thing and with the birth rates prevalent in Africa, any of these new and genuine countries that wish to increase its population can do as it pleases.

The only job that needs to be done is to identify the groups of viable countries that will emerge from the present Nigeria, collect signatures from each and approach the United Nations to conduct a referendum as was done for East Timor. The right to self determination is a right guaranteed by the United Nations to which Nigeria is a signatory. If the present national assembly was up to its responsibilities of representing the interest of those who elected it, this is what it should have done by now.

The second best option is to create these viable countries as autonomous states within a United States of Nigeria. The only thing that needs to be done is to identify the groups of autonomous language groups that will form the United States of Nigeria. This arrangement is a confederacy but one different from the confederacy that a majority of current politicians are demanding, namely, a confederation of the old four regions or the new six region grouping of Nigeria.

The third option, which I consider no option at all, in present day Nigeria, is to have what is, increasingly, being described as a true federation. A true federation only works in a country where there is a balance of power or terror between the federating units and where the spirit of democracy has become an ingrained culture. The only federating units in Nigeria which have any semblance of coherent and resilient unity, hence power, are the northern Muslims, the minorities such the Binis, the Efiks, the Tivs and to some extent the majority tribes of the Yorubas. All other groups make a lot of noise but have no credible leadership, follower-ship or cohesion. There is nowhere in Nigeria where genuine democracy is a culture or part of its history. That is, Nigeria, as presently constituted, cannot form a true federation.

## Resource Control and Income/Wealth Distribution

Resource control has been national problems since historic times but became prominent, in relation to individuals, because of socialism which came with the Bolshevik revolution of 1917, inspired by the writings of Karl Marx and Frederick Engels and the injustices and excesses of the Czars of Russia and spread to many countries dissatisfied with their rulers. The myths of Spartan socialism fuelled some of early Russian socialism until its unsuitability dawned on their protagonists. The myth of socialism is the ideal that the state is the best organ to control the productive resources of a nation as it is the only organ likely to distribute them fairly and equitably. Only fanatical socialists will refuse to see that this is what it is - an ideal – and not a feasible approach to the management of resources in a nation state. The big event of the twentieth century is the collapse of socialist states.

Amazingly, while Nigerian governments continue to practice old fashioned socialism, it claims to be practicing a mixed economy system while its socialist critics accuse it of practising capitalism. The fact is that the Nigerian government is practicing old fashioned socialism, by which it believes in, passes and enforces, laws which ensure that all natural resources and land in Nigeria belong to "all Nigerians", "all Nigerian", being in fact, the Nigerian federal government officials and their accomplices.

The truth, and this was the case before governments and nations came into being, is that whatever is found on your land belongs to you. The only thing government is entitled to, if you are a citizen of the country over which that government is in charge, is TAX, TAX and nothing but TAX, be it on income, consumption, excise or royalty, the rate which can be manipulated by government to achieve social and economic objectives. No government, federal, state or local, has any right to ownership of, or income from, any natural resource except in the form of tax. All one has to do is to look at the successful European and North American countries. These governments own nothing but have more resources from tax than any of the socialist countries which appropriate the wealth of their citizens.

Any national effort, even if it is a conference, (although this is what the national assembly is expected to have done by now) must, therefore, ensure that government is not involved in direct ownership of natural resources and land. We should learn from European and North American countries how they make laws on exploitation of natural resources and get tax from the owners. In our own case, having made the mistake, it can be rectified by capitalizing NNPC, Nigerian Coal Corporation and all government companies exploiting our natural resources, identifying individuals and communities (not governments whether state or local) on whose lands these resources were found, the fraction of resources or income from their land and allocating, proportionately, shares to them on the basis of the share value of the company. The present privatization exercise, proceeding at snail pace is, grossly, misdirected and fraudulent.

<u>Religion and Secularity in Nigeria</u>

Again, our leaders often delight in describing Nigeria as a multi-religious country and tout this as one of the signs of unity in diversity. It is only somebody who is either not conversant with, or concerned about, current affairs that will expect a country which has considerable populations of adherents of the two religions, Islam and Christianity, to live in peace or make any progress as a nation. History and even current day events are full of examples which show that the two can never live in peace in one country. There is never peace in a country with Muslims unless they are in charge. When they are in charge, there is never justice for non-Muslims until everybody is converted to Islam.

The agony that was Lebanon for many years is that the Christians there, coming from a long and ancient tradition, refused to be over-run. The only Muslim who brought respite in the war between Christians and Muslims has just been killed and Lebanon is back on its way to religious war. The Muslims in Nigeria have been getting away with all kinds of atrocities against Christians. The only time there is "peace" in Nigeria is when Christians absorb their atrocities and do not retaliate or become fanatical about their faith as the Muslims. When they become as fanatical as the Muslims, and they are being constantly provoked by even a government headed by a Christian, Nigeria will know no peace.

The 1999 and previous constitutions made all kinds of allowances to accommodate the Muslims. Yet they were not satisfied and saw everything not Muslim in origin or left by the colonialists (including the pagan calendar and naming of days of the week and months after their ancient gods) as Christian and once it is Christian, whether it is good or bad, it must either be destroyed or

Islamized. They were allowed to use non-Muslim fellow citizens' share of foreign exchange to go on Hajj and they see nothing wrong with it and even use state resources to encourage more people to go on Hajj. Nigeria is still a member of the OIC and they see nothing wrong with it. The justification is the false claim that Nigeria is an Islamic country with minority Christian population! And General Babangida (rtd.), who did all this, is angling to come back as President of Nigeria!

The northern states of Nigeria established Sharia law contrary to the Constitution and they are even claiming that the Constitution allows them to do that. Is that an honest way to relate to people of other faiths in the same country? Muslims in Nigeria will blaspheme against Christian beliefs, deny and ridicule the Christian Trinity and call Our Lord Jesus Christ a prophet, but once anything is said against prophet Mohamed, they kill and burn. It is clear that no definition of secularity will satisfy Nigerian Muslims until Nigeria is declared an Islamic republic. No country can be one or make progress once a considerable proportion of its citizens have this attitude. Not even if that country is a true federation or a confederation. It is irresponsible and unrealistic to keep hoping that this will change.

Perhaps it is fortunate that the nineteen northern states have embarked on full blown Sharia. These states could be the basis of one neighbouring Islamic republic that should be carved out of Nigeria. Other secular neighbouring countries can be carved out of the present south western, south-south, south eastern and north central states of Nigeria based on a referendum by the United Nations. A United States of Nigeria confederation which contains a Muslim member would be highly unstable.

<u>How can all these be done without a National Conference?</u>

For the reasons given earlier in this memorandum, a national conference, though attractive in concept, cannot succeed in present day Nigeria, without prolonged and sustained public education. Neither will any approach to tribal or ethnic leaders, the present crop of which is obsessed with self preservation. What will succeed, in my view, is a technical approach by a group or committee inspired by eminent personalities such as Chief Anthony Enahoro, Professor Wole Soyinka or similar, not a national conference, at least not now. I shall call this group or committee, the PRONACO group or committee

The first technical approach is to correct the false representation at the national assembly and the delineation of electoral constituencies. Going by the example of court judgements which are corrected whenever serious transcribing errors are detected, I suggest that the law on local government and constituency delineation predating the 1979 and 1999 Constitutions of Nigeria be re-visited by a small PRONACO committee. This committee will find the following anomalies:

1. Local governments in the south of Nigeria were not delineated according to the existing law, then, which stipulated among other things that no local government population should exceed 300,000, later revised down to 150,000. Thus the local governments listed in the 1999 constitution, for southern states, are illegal and need judicial correction, not a new law, to make each 150,000 or 300, 000 in population, depending on which figure was used for the 1999 Constitution.
2. Constituency delineation in southern states of Nigeria was, similarly, not done according to the then existing law regarding the population for each constituency. They, too, need judicial correction.

When these figures are confirmed and a legal number list of local government areas and constituencies for each southern, and northern, state is compiled, a demand should then be made, if necessary, by court action, for these judicial corrections to be effected and bye-elections to the new constituencies conducted. If this approach is successful, it will result in a more balanced and representative national assembly and distribution of national revenue.

The second technical approach is for a PRONACO committee to study ethnic identities and affiliations in present day Nigeria. Each ethnic group in Nigeria has a history of its origins, its uncles, aunts and cousins. Usually, their language or dialects are related and they understand each other. These are the entities that will form the basis of any negotiations, conferences, states or countries in any arrangement that results. This second approach can be pursued, simultaneously, with the first technical approach.

The third technical approach, which cannot be implemented unless the second technical approach is completed, is the decision stage when the PRONACO group, as a whole, note, not as committee, decides which option to pursue:

1. whether to start a public information and relations campaign in and outside Nigeria to enlighten the public and the world on the issues before embarking on any action
2. whether to approach each identified ethnic group for discussions on the way forward on the three main issues raised above
3. whether to start collecting signatures for presentation to the Nigerian national assembly to effect these changes
4. whether to start collecting signatures for presentation to the United nations to conduct a referendum to effect these changes

Conclusion

These suggestions appear to be separatist or secessionist. This is not the intention of this memorandum, even though these may turn out to be their consequence. Rather, they are what I consider to be a true situation analysis of our condition in Nigeria, indeed Africa. If we love ourselves and nation, we have to get out of the colonial blanket, apparently, but not really, welded to our skins and suffocating us. This blanket is the design by European countries, in pursuit of their commercial and political interests, to ensure that, in perpetuity, Africa is cocooned in unworkable, self destroying, agglomeration of incompatible ethnic groups which they label countries and give "independence".

It is the mandate and destiny of four or five generations, of which we are the current, which have had the opportunity to understudy, participate and experience these events in world and African history, to change the situation. If this succeeds in Nigeria, Africa will be free at last.

**Table 1: Population of African Countries mid-2004**

| Country | Population, Millions |
| --- | --- |
| Nigeria | 137.3 |
| Egypt | 76.1 |
| Ethiopia | 67.9 |
| Republic of the Congo | 58.3 |
| South Africa | 42.7 |
| Sudan | 39.2 |
| Tanzania | 36.6 |
| Morocco | 32.2 |
| Algeria | 32.1 |
| Kenya | 32.0 |
| Uganda | 26.4 |
| Ghana | 20.8 |
| Mozambique | 18.8 |
| Madagascar | 17.5 |
| Cote d'Ivoire | 17.3 |
| Cameroon | 16.1 |
| Burkina Faso | 13.6 |
| Zimbabwe | 12.7 |
| Mali | 12.0 |
| Malawi | 11.9 |
| Niger | 11.4 |
| Angola | 11.0 |
| Senegal | 10.9 |
| Zambia | 10.5 |

| | |
|---|---|
| Tunisia | 10.0 |
| Chad | 9.5 |
| Guinea | 9.3 |
| Somalia | 8.3 |
| Rwanda | 8.0 |
| Benin | 7.3 |
| Burundi | 6.2 |
| Sierra Leone | 5.9 |
| Libya | 5.6 |
| Togo | 5.6 |
| Eritrea | 4.5 |
| Central African Republic | 3.7 |
| Liberia | 3.4 |
| Democratic Republic of the Congo | 3.0 |
| Mauritania | 3.0 |
| Namibia | 2.0 |
| Lesotho | 1.9 |
| Botswana | 1.6 |
| The Gambia | 1.6 |
| Gabon | 1.4 |
| Guinea-Bissau | 1.4 |
| Mauritius | 1.2 |
| Swaziland | 1.2 |
| Comoros | 0.7 |
| Equatorial Guinea | 0.5 |
| Cape Verde | 0.4 |
| Western Sahara | 0.3 |
| Sao Tome & Principe | 0.2 |
| Seychelles | 0.08 |
| **Total Population of African Countries** | **873.08** |

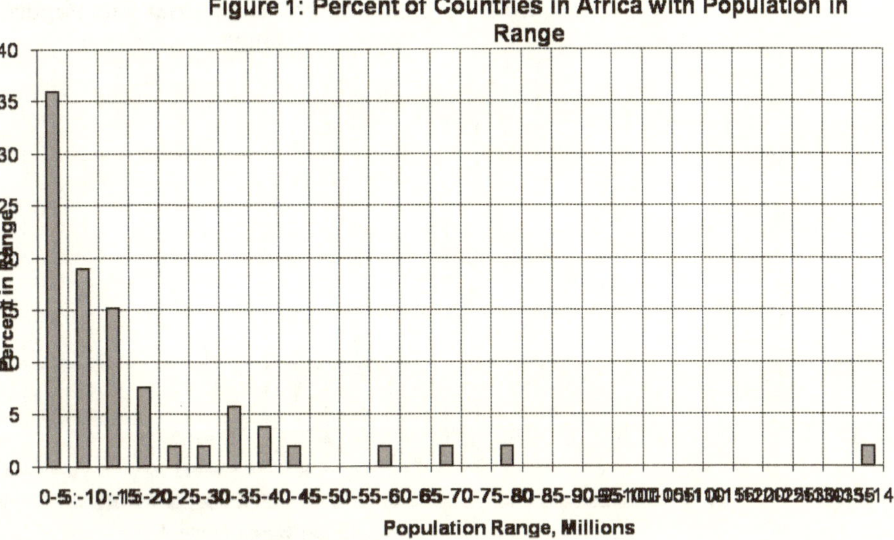

**Figure 1: Percent of Countries in Africa with Population in Range**



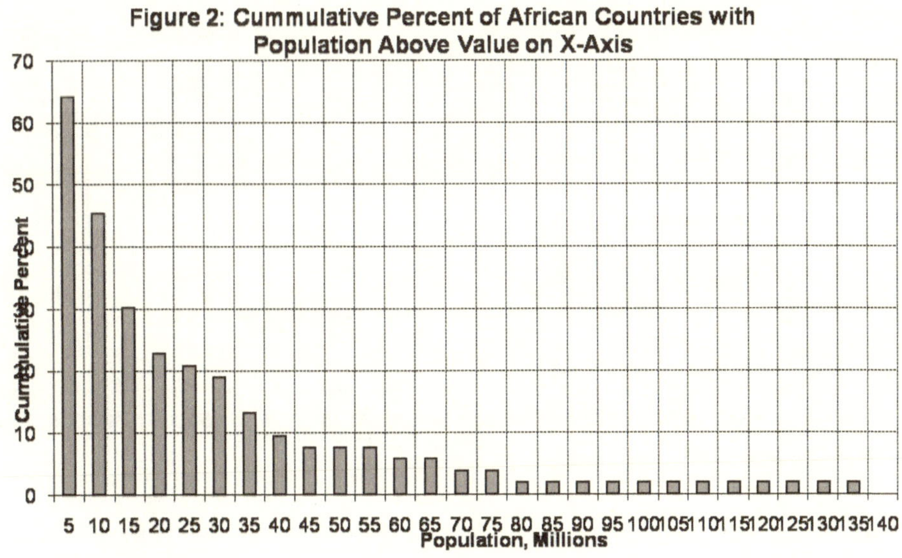

**Figure 2: Cummulative Percent of African Countries with Population Above Value on X-Axis**



29

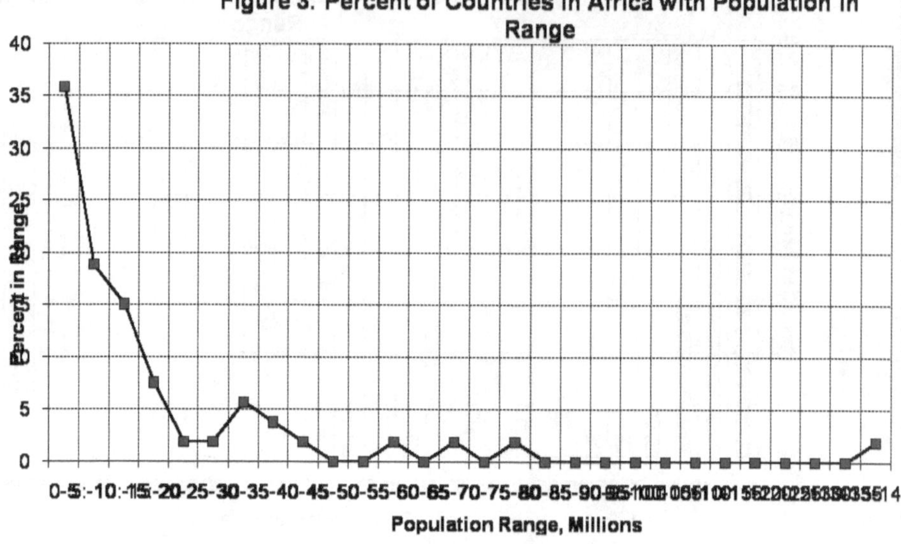

Figure 3: Percent of Countries in Africa with Population in Range

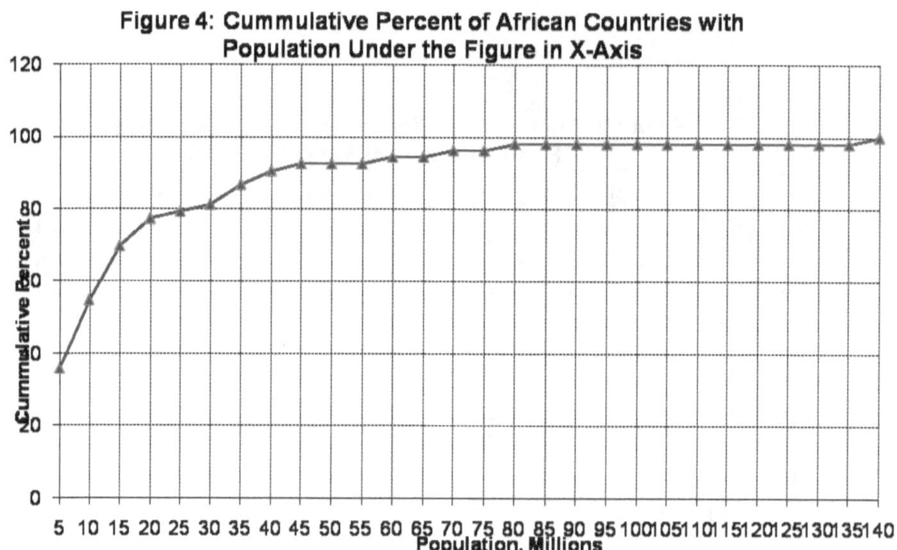

Figure 4: Cummulative Percent of African Countries with Population Under the Figure in X-Axis

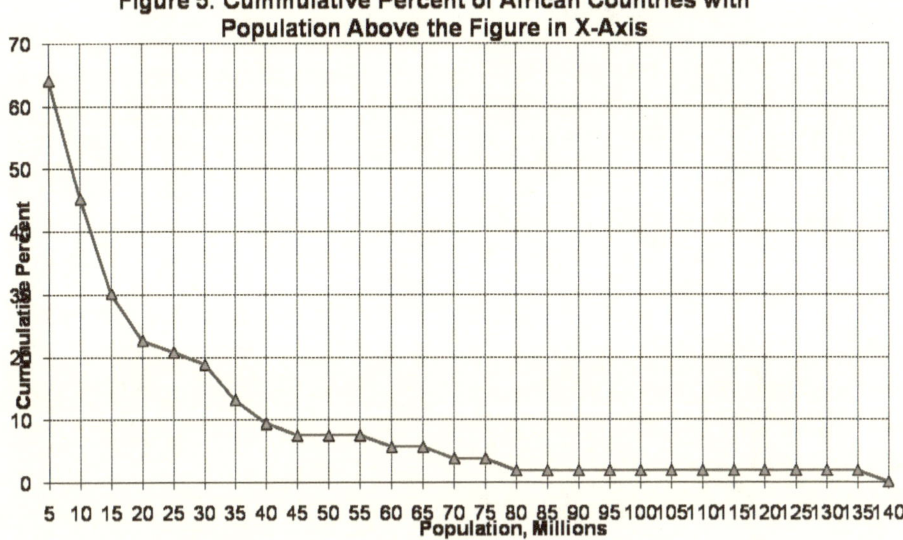

**Figure 5: Cummulative Percent of African Countries with Population Above the Figure in X-Axis**